Lonesome Man on a Hermit's Hill
A Verse Play

Edward Kenny

Bluebird Publishing—Lindenhurst, NY
ISBN: 978-0578604862
Lonesome Man on a Hermit's Hill
Edward Kenny
Available formats: eBook | paperback distribution
Contact: bluebirdsongspub@gmail.com

Acknowledgements

For my parents.

Edited by Christopher Kenny

Forward

Lonesome Man on a Hermit's Hill was also written as a musical stage play by Edward Kenny. It is presented here as verse play.

CAST OF CHARACTERS
In Order of Appearance

MARION'S AND NEIL'S PARENTS (Offstage in a flashback)

MARION………………A farmer, sister of Neil

NEIL …………………..A farmer and underground revolutionary

IAN ……………………A reclusive poet

BRIANNA……………..Neil's lover

DEVLIN……………….A leprechaun who appears only to Ian

GENERAL BRIGGS ….An English General

The Story

Imagine a man living in Ireland in the 1800s, who desperately wants to be sane and to socialize with his neighbors, but is restricted from fulfilling those desires by his propensity to see, hear, and converse with leprechauns. Imagine that the same man is a talented, albeit, reclusive poet, who seeks to improve the plight of his starving countrymen, through the power of his pen, but has not of yet lent his talents to political advocacy. Rather than speak in public, even to offer a reading of his poetry, the man remains aloof, pretending that drink is the source of the hallucinations that others know he has and that he knows he cannot separate from reality. The man is Ian, the personification of the *Lonesome Man on a Hermit's Hill*.

Perceptions of this solitary poet vary. The more common view is that held by Neil, Ian's underground revolutionary neighbor, who sees him as an inconsequential minor celebrity in the face of a famine that engulfs the region, compounded by the corruption of the occupying British army, led by General Briggs. Neil's sister, Marion, is in the minority in her romantic infatuation with Ian, which is a source of irritation to her protective and idealistic brother. Little does Marion know that Ian shares her feelings, but cannot reciprocate, even with a word or a smile, ashamed of his unwanted entourage of "little people."

What Ian, Neil and Marion have in common is that they were all orphaned by an earlier famine. Over time, Neil recognizes in Ian an opportunity to use his writing talent to inspire, grow and mobilize the revolutionary movement against the tyranny of the crown. Ian's spirit is willing, but his emotional ability to fulfill this calling is undermined by the persistent presence of the leprechauns, led by the diabolical Devlin.

And so, Ian fails in his attempt to become the voice of the revolution, at least until circumstances change. When Neil is betrayed by his lover, the vixen Brianna, he is imprisoned by General Briggs, an action that humiliates Ian, devastates Marion, and threatens the survival of the underground movement against the army.

What happens next unfolds in this exciting, lyrical, and romantic story about hunger, starvation, imperialism, courage and the power of love to overcome all odds, all presented in verse by Edward Kenny. Read and discover the destiny of the *Lonesome Man on a Hermit's Hill*.

ENTRE ACT

Before the curtain rises, images of the Great Irish
Famine are projected as the parents of MARION and
NEIL speak offstage.

FATHER
From the hellacious heat of the summer,
On the day the last flower would die,
Comes the rainfall that flooded the clover,
Like the tears that the widows would cry.

MOTHER
When the work of the day would be over,
And the darkness would fall on the bog,
Like the shroud of a witch it would cover
All the fields with a blue colored fog.

FATHER
Down in the ground were planted the praties,
So, we dug them and searched through the stack,
For food to replace what the snow buries,
But no, all the potatoes were black.

MOTHER
Whether visits of providence happen,
As punishment for food that we waste,
Or the faeries are using a weapon,
Once it's gone, a crop can't be replaced.

BOTH
Can you spare a crumb?
Just a bite or two?
Just a sliver of
What God gave to you?
Would you turn us out?
From our cottage home,
To live in a scalp,
Or be left to roam?
We would gladly work,
Even with no meal,
But in workhouse filth,
Now, how would you feel?
And how could we watch
Our own children die?
And so, for their sake,
We say our goodbye.

FATHER
And of man do we learn in disaster,
Some will sacrifice for those in need,
But then, others enslave to be master,
Evicting, starving, to feed their greed.

MOTHER
First the farmers put out those who labor,
Then the landlords show them how to steal,
The monarchy could be the savior,
But serves politics instead of a meal.

BOTH
Can you spare a crumb?
Just a bite or two?

Just a sliver of
What God gave to you?
Would you turn us out?
From our cottage home,
To live in a scalp,
Or be left to roam?
We would gladly work,
Even with no meal,
But in workhouse filth,
Now, how would you feel?
And how could we watch
Our own children die?
And so, for their sake,
We say our goodbye.

(The projection ends and the theatre is dark until the curtain opens.)

ACT I

Scene 1

SETTING: It is the summer in the nineteenth century, on a farm in County Mayo, Ireland. A small road passes the farm which is bordered by a white picket fence. Just inside the fence is a small, simple farmhouse. Next to the farmhouse is a potato field.

AT RISE: The owners of the farm, NEIL and his sister MARION, are working in the potato field. Although they are in their late 20's, they appear weathered for their years as the result of barely surviving a famine, which left them to manage the farm as orphaned children. Now, more than ten years later, a new famine has begun, the product of a potato blight. NEIL has become an underground revolutionary, fighting for what he perceives to be the political causes of hunger and poverty in Ireland, and the English occupation as well. His sister is more the romantic, and as such, is smitten by a wealthy, and apparently, heavy drinking reclusive poet, IAN, who lives in a mansion on a hill just up the road. After an offstage narration by IAN, the action flashes back to an afternoon when IAN was passing the farm on the way to his home.

IAN (O.S.)
The old house was somehow different then. It stood like a hollow shell, a ghost ship atop the green sea of

clover that once was my family's hill. A dirt road led me back from the village to my home. The road weaved its way like a thread between the seams of heaven and hell. In that time and place, the two were sewn dangerously close to one another. As I reached the foot of the hill, I would often see Marion and her brother, Neil, working in the furrowed fields. Her eyes were the windows through which I would see the heavenly side of this Emerald Isle. Like all the rest, they thought they knew me: a reclusive poet who thought he could talk to the little people, and a slave to whiskey. They couldn't know that I was trapped inside a different glass, inside a bottle of emotion. And so, I wrote my poems, and I carried a bottle to perpetrate the drinking myth. It was that lie which enabled me to remain mute, but for my poems. And yet, even that voice was growing faint. Oh, I wanted to speak out for love, and for justice, but I was fighting a demon of my own. And I didn't need to drink to see a leprechaun.

MARION
(As his off-stage narration ends, IAN enters.
MARION leaves her work to speak with IAN.
He hesitates, but repeatedly avoids her.)

They say you were born in a mystical place
To a woman who had an angel's face,
And a father who held you upon his knee.
They gave you the wind, the stars and the sea.

They gave you the shamrock and the golden sod,
A family's love, and the word of God.

And they rise like the sun in your memory,
They're the spring and fall of your poetry.

Oh, lonesome man on a hermit's hill,
Speak ye now or you never, ever will
Write a poem for the suffering souls,
It's for the likes of us that the church bell tolls.

Now I speak of these things, not to bring you pain,
For a flower to grow it must see rain.
You were given the world of the leprechaun,
But when the famine came, your world was gone.

MARION
Now all but their spirits lies beneath a stone
But their spirits are out in the unknown.
And so, you go on but won't utter a word,
While the child in you cries out to be heard.

Oh, lonesome man on a hermit's hill,
Speak ye now or you never, ever will.
Write a poem for the suffering souls,
It's for the likes of us that the church bell tolls.

(IAN pauses as if about to speak, but then
hurriedly turns and EXITS as NEIL approaches
MARION angrily.)

NEIL
You waste your time
Talking to a fool
There's more sense at
The back of a mule.

MARION
The wee people raised him!

NEIL
This man's no man,
A man without a cause.

MARION
(Shouting in exasperation)
He's an artist.

NEIL
(Equally exasperated)
And I was a baron!
Your work of art.
It is filled with flaws.

MARION
Look, you drive him away,
Just as he was to speak!
Can't you see that someone
Besides you is unique?

NEIL
So, let him go
Hide inside his home,
While soldiers fight
He can write a poem.

MARION
It's not your place,
My life is my own.

NEIL
I'm flesh and blood,
Soon you'll see the bone.
We will all be starving,
Unless we can revolt!
If you must find romance,
Then first find an adult!

MARION
He's not a child,
Just an innocent.
A man of peace,
Why won't you consent?

NEIL
My sister, dear,
There's no innocence.
The middle ground
Stands at our expense.

While England is hoarding
All the food that we need,
Rather than stand and starve,
By a bullet I'll bleed.

(Neil turns to exit in anger.)

MARION
Neil please don't leave
'Til you clear your mind.
You're good, you're wise,
Anger makes you blind.

You think they can't catch you
In a trap,
They're bound to find weakness
To tap.

NEIL
(Getting in the last word)
There's no time to argue
All the pros and cons,
But I'm not so crazy
To talk to leprechauns!

(NEIL motions with his finger to his head to
indicate that IAN is crazy, then he EXITS.
MARION steps down in one.)

MARION
Acting out this drama
That exists between us two,
Speaking lines to cover
What we know is true.

There has been a secret
That has never been discussed.
It concerns a woman,
One day she'll betray your trust.

And where you've been going,
It is not to see a friend,
Oh, I know the story
And I fear how it will end.

MARION
Momentary passion,
And a treacherous embrace,
Words that you've forgotten
Oh, a time, a name, a place.

And it's the irony of ironies,
You can criticize me all you please.
And you can disavow the man I choose,
Still I can't seem to give you the news.

You have been the elder,
Wise protector all along,
My mother and father,
When so much was going wrong.

We survived a famine.
When you were yourself a child,
And with your tears inside,
For my sake you always smiled.

Now you are a rebel,
And one nation is your cause.
But she's made you careless
And you can't afford such flaws.

You're living in danger,
Now it's you I should protect,
But I'm left to cower
Out of fear of disrespect.

And it's the irony of ironies,
You can criticize me all you please,

And you can disavow the man I choose
Still I can't seem to give you the news.

(Looking back in the direction of where
NEIL exited)

MARION
I'll tell him tomorrow
And just for tonight I'll pray,
That his secret lover
Won't give his secrets away.

(She exits.)

NEIL
(NEIL enters and is spotlighted, as he walks
down the road, away from MARION.)
My nightmare will come true the day,
I see my sister below the steeple,
Marrying he who was raised,
Or so she thinks, by the little people.

(He exits.)

(End of Scene 1.)

ACT I

Scene 2

SETTING: Flashback to the yard outside of IAN's Mansion. He is only a boy, about eight years old. He is playing alone when a group of LEPRECHAUNS enter, performing a step dance and playing with him in a friendly manner. DEVLIN is their leader.

LEPRECHAUNS
Pat pitter pat pitter patter.
Like a torrent of rain in the street,
Not that a storm is approaching,
But the steps of the tiniest feet.

DEVLIN
If you mistake them for children,
You will think that it's terribly weird,
When you squint your eyes and see one
Who's undoubtedly sporting a beard.

LEPRECHAUNS
Pat pitter pat pitter patter,
It's so strange who a person can meet,
Under the moon of the highway
When he's looking for something to eat.

DEVLIN
Seldom a mortal will see them,
Sure, the moor played a trick with eyes,

Except if he was an orphan
With no one else to answer his cries.

LEPRECHAUNS
And we slide down the side of a rainbow,
We give you our mischief, you give us your gold,
But were it not for the little people,
The children abandoned would starve in the cold.

Down to the heart of the matter,
We're the souls who were left all alone,
Neglected or forgotten,
We're the ghosts who take care of our own.

DEVLIN
We know all about starvation,
So, we've befriended many a child,
And the first time I met Ian
Was the first time in years that he smiled.

LEPRECHAUNS
And we slide down the side of a rainbow,
We give you our mischief, you give us your gold,
But were it not for the little people
The children abandoned would starve in the cold.

(End of Scene 2)

ACT I

Scene 3

SETTING: In the evening of the same day. NEIL ENTERS BRIANNA'S cottage. They kiss passionately.

BRIANNA
I've been elusive to the average man,
And yet their women see some master plan.
They see a vixen, who is to be feared,
Recount disasters that I've engineered.

But like a tiger, you were born to tame,
I drew you closer, through a ring of flame.
For your desire, you took a chance,
Now we're together in a mating dance.

And it's conclusive you're no average man,
For I scratch the back of a partisan
Who lifts me up from the life I disdain
As pleasure opens up the clouds again.

We roll like thunder in a changing sky,
In flashing lightning, I can catch your eye,
And each emotion I've ever felt
Explodes inside of me, until I melt.

And so, I need you to be
The river by my side,
To flow through me with passion,

And take me for a ride.
Though it may be dangerous,
On downward I will slide,
Because I need you to be
The river by my side.

NEIL
A flight of fancy for the mortal man,
You are the woman of their master plan.
You're the reason why the minstrel sings,
A worthy consort in the land of kings.

But ever since I lost my royalty
I've been in search of my nobility.
The kind that sees that everyone is fed,
That children have a roof overhead.

BRIANNA
Yes, I know and you're a shining knight.

NEIL
I'm only trying to make what's wrong right.

BRIANNA
You're not a statue that's made of stone
We're only human when we're all alone.

NEIL
We roll like thunder in a changing sky.

BRIANNA
And each emotion that I've ever felt
Explodes inside of me until I melt.

NEIL
And so, I need you to be
The river by my side.

BRIANNA
To flow through me with passion,
And take me for a ride.

NEIL
Though it may be dangerous,
On downward I will slide,
Because I need you to be
The river by my side.

(NEIL kisses her quickly and then begins to exit.)

BRIANNA
                (Seductively)
Where are you going?
Why don't you stay the night?
You would be safe here,
We'll lay low out of sight.

NEIL
     (Pulling away gently)
I have given some people my word.
We must find a way to be heard.

 BRIANNA
Is it your sister?
That she doesn't like me?

NEIL
No. She's too busy
With that hermit's poetry.
    (illuminated with an idea.)
But perhaps that's the answer at last,
Poems communicate feelings fast.

BRIANNA
What are you saying?
What he writes is absurd.

NEIL
Yet some people live
And they die on each word.

BRIANNA
        (Trying to restrain him.)
Where are you going?
Maybe I'll tag along.

NEIL
See you tomorrow,
Stay here where you belong.
I have given some people my word.

(They kiss and NEIL EXITS.)

Fade to black.

(End of Scene 3.)

ACT I

Scene 4

SETTING: Also, that same evening, IAN is alone inside his mansion on a hill.

IAN
He doesn't think that I can hear her,
He thinks me deaf, he thinks me dumb,
He doesn't know I long to be near her,
Or how I loathe what I've become.

I want to fall into her eyes
And find a love that never dies.
I know that chance will not come twice,
Such love I've traded for my vice.

He doesn't see when I am dreaming,
He thinks me weak, he thinks me lame,
He doesn't hear inside me screaming,
Or see this beast I've tried to tame.

Though I've been the winner many nights,
After courageous bloody fights,
More times I've felt its claws of ice,
My pride, I've traded for my vice.

She doesn't read the words I write her,
She thinks me mild, she thinks me meek.
She doesn't know me as a fighter,

But with my pen I fight to speak.

There is a tempest in my soul,
Held in my secret friend's control.
But I will see it in defeat,
Or I will die and be complete.

For I remember yesterday,
The Emerald Isle where I would play,
It wasn't worth the sacrifice,
The life I've traded for my vice.

(ENTER DEVLIN and the LEPRECHAUNS,
behind IAN.)

DEVLIN
There's a creak,
There's a crack.
There are eyes
At your back,
And they're staring.

So you twist,
And you turn,
And you try
To discern
Who is glaring.

Are there ghosts
Hereabout?
You believe,
Then you doubt
Your own senses.

Without kin,
I came in
To begin
Wearing thin
Your defenses.

(IAN is upset by what his imagination
 is conjuring)

LEPRECHAUNS
But everyone's got a potential pot of gold,
A little trinket of a secret that they hold.
And just when you think you've found it,
Suddenly it's gone,
You never blame yourself,
you blame the leprechaun.

'Tis himself,
Look who's here.
Come on boys
And appear
To the master.

He's our man,
He believes
We're the tricks
Up his sleeves
Through disaster.

In his mind
We're the charms
To defeat
Any arms

On the outside.

So alone,
Stands this stone,
An unknown
Broken bone
On the inside.

(IAN tries to walk away from and turn
 his back on DEVLIN. DEVLIN keeps
 jumping in front of him.)

LEPRECHAUNS
But everyone's got a potential pot of gold,
A little trinket of a secret that they hold.
And just when you think you've found it,
Suddenly it's gone,
You never blame yourself, you blame the leprechaun.

At the end
Of his dream,
Straight he walks
To a beam,
And he's plastered.

(While trying to elude DEVLIN, IAN
 inadvertently walks into a beam, then
 collapses.)

DEVLIN
And then puff!
Our job's done!
Sun is up,

It was fun
While it lasted.

We live by
Your belief,
It's not us,
Time's the thief
That's intruding.

At your door
With a thump
Then you feel
What a bump
Is intruding.

LEPRECHAUNS
But everyone's got a potential pot of gold,
A little trinket of a secret that they hold.
And just when you think
That you've found it, suddenly it's gone.
You never blame yourself, you blame the leprechaun.
It's too bad
Kind of sad,
Mom and Dad,
All you had,
Now, has traveled on

DEVLIN
They will think
It's the drink,
I won't tell
I'll just wink. . .
Matters not

What they think . . .
Blame it on . . .
Blame it on
The leprechaun.

(End of scene 4)

ACT I

Scene 5

SETTING: The following morning, in their farmhouse, NEIL wakes MARION. She dresses during the scene, and NEIL leads her out of the house, up the hill, to where IAN lives.

NEIL
There is little that is honest
While pursuing an extreme,
But perhaps there is a token
We can share and then redeem.

To be fighting for the Irish,
To give their life quality,
It's a means but not an ending,
For my life is you and me.

MARION
There it is, now, my dear brother,
Sure as my blood's in your vein,
A better life for your sister,
That is what you hope to gain.

But we're grown, and I'm a woman,
And my life's in my own hands,
I see love instead of famine
And my poet understands.

Sometimes you have to be your own best friend,
Selfish, yes, but true to the end.
Sometimes you stand alone in a crowd,
Silent when the voices are loud.

NEIL
Do you plan to live on loving
After this potato blight?
Will your poet write to England
To stand up for what is right?

MARION
Just like us, he is an orphan,
The last famine took his kin.

NEIL
He's a fool to believe them that
Hoarded food and medicine.

MARION
'Though I've had so little romance,
He's unlike the men I've seen,
To him ours is not a country,
It's a star of emerald green.

NEIL
Sad to say his star is fading,
He's been writing without themes,
When a star shuts out the public,
There's no purpose to his dreams.

(They find the door to Ian's house ajar and
enter. MARION and NEIL do not notice

DEVLIN as he enters to SPEAK.)

DEVLIN
Sometimes you count on a friend for luck,
Foolishly you forget to duck.
Sometimes your luck takes a negative roll,
'cause you left your friend in control.

(DEVLIN hides from view of NEIL and MARION.)

MARION
(Speaking to NEIL as they enter the room where
IAN is lying unconscious.)
Despite all our disagreements,
My love for you is profound.

NEIL
Well, I second that position,
And propose some common ground.

You've been a sister and daughter,
But you've never been a wife,
You should match up with a partner
Who has meaning to his life.

I am speaking of your poet,
And the power of his word.
It could galvanize the people
From the moment it is heard.

MARION
That would put him into danger.

NEIL
Without danger what's life worth?
I'm giving him a purpose…

(NEIL continues to walk through the room and
turns a chair around revealing IAN laying un-
conscious. MARION looks at IAN with forlorn
 affection. NEIL pantomimes drinking
from a bottle and points to IAN. They both
think that IAN is sleeping off a night of
drinking.)

MARION
Will he serve it on this earth?

(NEIL and MARION try to awaken IAN.)
NEIL
Time to pick your head off the floor
And read between the planks.
When you'll soon be caught up in a war,
It's time to choose your ranks.

You can sit there sucking on your thumb
But one day you will find,
'though they believe you're deaf and dumb,
They know you aren't blind.

Once you learn not choosing is a choice,
You'll have to take a stand.
Why not make poetry a voice
To speak throughout the land?

(IAN is now awake, but acts a little groggy.)

MARION
IAN, I see Ireland in you,
Imprisoned by the past.
Your wealth came from writing what you knew,
But that world didn't last.

Don't you see it is as clear?
It is as clear as wrong and right?
Don't you see it is the same?
It is the same potato blight?

NEIL
In the workhouse on the dole,
That's the only way we will eat.
First the body, then the soul,
That is how they'll ensure defeat.

There are names which bear a coat of arms,
For the battles they've won.
But it's "an idea" that helps or harms
Much more than any gun.
It seems we lose even when we win
With violence you see.
If you'd fight beside me with your pen
We'd share the victory.

MARION AND NEIL
(To NEIL)
Don't you see it is as clear?
It is as clear as wrong and right?
Don't you see it is the same?
It is the same potato blight?

NEIL
In the workhouse on the dole,
That's the only way we will eat.
First the body, then the soul,
That is the how they'll ensure defeat.

(Sensing that the others aren't on their guard,
DEVLIN exits silently.)

Say goodbye to your little friends
Who live inside your glass.
The fate of the hungry now depends
On your courage and class.

Come tonight to meet us at the pub,
We're orphans just like you.
If before we've given you the snub,
Tonight, we'll start anew.

MARION AND NEIL
Don't you see it is as clear?
It is as clear as wrong and right?
Don't you see it is the same?
It is the same potato blight?

NEIL
In the workhouse, on the dole,
That's the only way we will eat.
First the body, then the soul,
That's how they'll ensure our defeat.

Time to pick your head up off the floor,
Your parents would be proud.

London locked their food up in the store,
While starving was allowed.

(IAN is now alert and nods in response
to NEIL.)

NEIL
I know I will see you there,
I will see you there tonight.
Yes, just one poem in your name
Could change the same potato blight.

(MARION and NEIL EXIT. IAN rises,
  washes his face and changes his shirt.)

IAN
It's true I've watched my destiny
Go up in smoke.
I've made my life a travesty,
A stale old joke.
But here's my opportunity
To shed this cloak,
To even serve humanity
In one bold stroke.

(He holds a paper and quill pen.)

Yes, I will use my poetry
To tell the tale
About hunger and poverty.
I will prevail.

IAN
(continued)
So not another family
Will have to choke.
And I'll find freedom, finally,
In one bold stroke.

(He throws away the paper and quill.)

Why, like a snail in a shell,
Do I slow down to a crawl?
Why do I slip back to hell
When I tried not to fall?
Locking myself inside a cage
I can feel myself sink
Down onto an empty page
Until I cannot think.

(He falls to his knees.)

I dreamed once in a fantasy
Of my kin folk.
I'd teach the world of their history,
Not be some bloke
Who becomes just a comedy,
While his tears soak
Away his pride and sanity . . .
In one bold stroke.

(IAN covers his face with his hands.)

(Fade to black)

(End of scene 5)

ACT I

Scene 6

SETTING: Later that same day. GENERAL BRIGGS is marching down the main road past the farmhouse with his COMPANY.

GENERAL BRIGGS
An insurrection here,
A revolution there,
Society left to the ravages
Wrought by leniency on savages,
Whose movement underground
Devaluates the pound,
While they secretly spread their sedition
All under the guise of malnutrition.

COMPANY
       (marching in place)
We can't have the economy in anarchy!
We can't give any colony autonomy!
Where the shamrock is too high we will cut it down,
For we must preserve another jewel in the Crown.

BRIGGS
They rob to feed the land,
Wreck supply and demand.
With prices falling on commodities,
The empire could lose its properties.
Who profits from the deal?

The locals here who steal!
If they establish their democracy,
What will become of aristocracy?

COMPANY
          (marching in place)
We can't have the economy in anarchy!
We can't give any colony autonomy!
Where the shamrock is too high we will cut it down.
For we must preserve another jewel in the crown.

BRIGGS
We'll form the British square
And then the crowd will clear,
And we will go marching on imperially,
Bringing this soil back to sovereignty.

So where is this Neil bloke?
For once we clear the smoke.
We will show him to those who persevere
And demonstrate how troubles disappear.

COMPANY
          (marching in place)
We can't have the economy in anarchy!
We can't give any colony autonomy!
Where the shamrock is too high we will cut it down,
For we must preserve another jewel in the crown.

(They EXIT.)

(End of scene 6.)

ACT I

Scene 7

SETTING: That evening NEIL holds a secret meeting in a pub.

NEIL
I thought how I would come here,
Just to meet with my friends,
I saw how it all started,
Now I'll see how it ends.

(the PATRONS gather to listen)

I envisioned this movement,
As a tree that would grow,
As I nurtured the branches,
There was no way to know.

It seems somehow we've all been betrayed,
It seems someone's played a masquerade.
When I see them I won't have to ask,
I will know the eyes behind the mask.

I see the British army.
They've surrounded the town.
And it's all for one person,
Such a man of renown.

But why are they not searching?

You'd expect door to door.
They seem to know his pattern,
Like they've watched him before.

It seems somehow we've all been betrayed. It
seems someone's played a masquerade. When
I see them, I won't have to ask,
I will know the eyes behind the mask.

They say to go underground.
There is no time to spare,
(looking over his shoulder as if hoping
IAN will arrive.)
But I wait for a poet,
Thinking that he'll be here.

I thought he'd write a message
To rhyme throughout the earth,
But he sleeps in a corner,
Just as before his birth.

They say to go underground,
And then, not to stay still.
But first I'll go see Brianna,
And say goodbye until . . .

And she'll speak to my sister,
For I'd bring danger there.
But I say keep your courage,
We will not fall to fear.

(ENTER General BRIGGS with his
MEN and BRIANNA, who is wearing a mask.)

NEIL
It seems somehow we've all been betrayed. It
seems someone's played a masquerade.

BRIANNA
Someday you'll know what I did was right.

BRIGGS
Locked in a prison far out of sight.

NEIL
It seems I'm the one who's been betrayed,
But was it only a masquerade?
(looking into BRIANNA's eyes.)
When I see you, I don't have to ask,
I can see your eyes behind the mask.

(The soldiers exit with NEIL in irons. The
GENERAL remains in the pub to drink ale.
As he does, he speaks to BRIANNA and any-
one else who will listen.)

GENERAL BRIGGS
The King and Queen demand results,
The kind that quickly catapults
Them into glory.
It's an old story.

Look back at what we've colonized
The savages we've civilized
Into loyalty
To the royalty.

But now they say I've grown too big for my britches,
no,
Well now, perhaps just a small amount.
And I must admit I'd like to share the riches,
And invest them in my own account

Now there's a place for politics,
The eloquence and magic tricks
Turned by the squires
Who start the fires.

But when the city's burning down,
Who dashes in and saves the crown,
Absent the credit?
Not I, you said it?

But now they say I've got only one agenda, no,
But then duty, sometimes I scoff it.
And my report may leave out all the addenda,
Pertaining to all of my profit.

The King and Queen build empires
Knowing full well that task requires
A great general,
And it always will!

There always will be sacrifice,
The conquered people pay the price.
First, we enslave them,
So, we can save them.

But now they say I'm just a mercenary, no,
Well now, perhaps yes, to some small degree,

I have my own system for the monetary,
Called one for England and one for me.

(End of Scene 7)

ACT I

Scene 8

SETTING: On the evening of the following day, NEIL is alone in a dark jail cell. Each character is spotlighted as they speak. IAN looks out the window at his house; MARION looks out the window at her farmhouse. DEVLIN is with IAN, though neither acknowledges the other.

NEIL
Now the room is dark,
And my thoughts are cold.
Will I see the sun
Before I grow old?

IAN
Now my soul is black.
Once it was like gold.
Will it shine again
As the days unfold?

MARION
'Though I feel the pain,
I will try to cope.
For I can't exist
If I lose all hope.

DEVLIN
Just a little luck

Will be all we need.
Grows a mighty tree
From a tiny seed.

ALL
Another chance,
And that is all we'll ask.
Another chance,
And we will meet the task.
Another chance,
And we will right the wrong,
To raise one voice in song,
For Ireland.

BRIGGS
            (standing outside of NEIL's cell)
Now the battle's won,
It's time to submit.
Now your fighter's down,
You might as well quit.

BRIANNA
(from the window of her cottage)
Yes, the battle's lost,
But remains the war.
If one man is down,
There must be one more.

ALL
Another chance,
And that is all we'll ask.
Another chance,
And we will meet the task.

Another chance,
And we will right the wrong,
To raise one voice in song,
For Ireland.

NEIL
There's a common dream
We share to be free,
For this magic place,
To find unity.

IAN
It's the force of God,
No man can reverse. Ireland
has its place
In the universe.

ALL
Another chance,
And that is all we ask,
Another chance,
And we will meet the task.
Another chance,
And we will right the
wrong, To raise one voice in
song, For Ireland.

(End of Act I.)

ACT II

Scene 1

<u>SETTING</u>: It is fall, late in the afternoon at an English workhouse in County Mayo.

<u>AT</u> <u>RISE</u>: The workhouse is dreary and empty except for a few people dressed in rags, wearily shoveling grain into canvas bags, closing the bags and stacking them into piles. MARION is among the workers.

WORKERS
You work and work
And what is there to show?
Another day,
Another foot below.

The very soil
Where you once sowed a seed
Is barren now,
Except for what you bleed.

And even that
Grows thinner every day,
Your face and name
Begin to fade away.

You work and work,
And never seem to stop.

You work and work
Because you lost a crop.

You work and work
Upon the public dole,
You lose your pride,
Your heart, and then your soul.

Who holds the pen that writes the plan?
Who gives the orders to that man?
How can they see reality
Inside the realm of royalty?

You work and work,
It cuts you like a knife.
To see them make
Slaves of your kids and wife.

You barely sleep
Or eat enough to live.
But still you pray
For the strength to forgive.

The ones who gain
From each one here that toils,
Whose politics
Reap all the workhouse spoils.

You want to work
And not take from their hand,
You want to work,
But work on your own land.

You work and work,
But still you have no voice.
You work and work,
Because you have no choice.

Who holds the pen that writes the plan?
Who gives the orders to that man?
How can they see reality
Inside the realm of royalty?

(ENTER GENERAL BRIGGS with IAN
in irons.)

FIRST WORKER
Look who it is gracing us with his presence.
For the source of our troubles
We don't have to look far.
They say of you, General Briggs,
That you're not fit to eat with the pigs.
We all agree that you are.

(the WORKERS laugh derisively.)

SECOND WORKER
Look who it is facing us all in silence.
You can take out a bottle
And then watch him succumb.
He could have helped our cause with a poem,
But, instead, he fell asleep at home,
Living alone, deaf and dumb.

(the WORKERS mutter angrily.)

49

MARION
But what of my brother?

Look how we've fallen behind in his absence . . .
Three years in the workhouse
Is a burden to bear,
But how long can I sanely survive
Not knowing if Neil's dead or alive?
(to BRIGGS)
It's time you made his fate clear!

BRIGGS
Everything will be clear to you in time.
(sarcastically, under his breath.)
From the ridiculous to the sublime.
Until then rather than going berserk,
(crossly)
Why don't you just get back to work?

IAN
        (to the workers)
All the past welling up inside of me,
Now at last I'll set those feelings free,
And, despite all the internal violence
In this time and place, I'll break the silence.

FIRST WORKER
But what of her brother?

SECOND WORKER
Look who it is breaking the years of silence!
But why didn't you help us
Back when you had the chance?

We wanted to communicate
To the world of our impending fate.
But you wrote about romance.

IAN
Ever since then I have suffered in silence,
It was never the bottle,
But the leprechaun inside.
'til I gave away all that I had
To feed and clothe those who think me mad.
I'm here to work by their side.
MARION
But what of your fortune?

IAN
        (downstage, in one.)
It's become a distant moment
And a fleeting glimpse of youth,
Long before the lies would foment,
And I'd finally learn the truth.

I was weaned on mythic stories,
Soon my own tales would be told
Of the little people's glories
And I made a pot of gold.

Oh, my friends, I am so sorry.
I was lost within myself.
And I've locked up all my feelings
In a book upon a shelf.

Pass the tales of generations,
Just like passing a baton,

'Til you wake up at last one morning,
All the leprechauns are gone.

They enchanted me with magic,
But the years then slowly filed,
And their figures became tragic,
When I was no more a child.

And with all the adults dying
You would think they'd disappear.
But I heard the banshee's crying,
And I kept my wee friends near.

Oh, my friends, my friends, I'm sorry.
I was lost within myself.
And I've locked up all my feelings
In a book upon a shelf.

Pass the tales of generations
Just like passing a baton
'Til you wake up at last one morning,
All the leprechauns are gone.

IAN
(continued)
When you can't accept the vision
Of an endless sky of rain,
You use your imagination
To see rainbows once again.

But I left my playmates' prison
On the night I cast them out.
Along with them went my fortune,

Now I will pay your way out.

Oh, my friends, you have your freedom,
Though I can't replace what's lost.
Now the poems I've sold have meaning,
And my childhood isn't lost.

Pass them on through generations,
Just like passing a baton,
At last I'll be out of mourning,
All the leprechauns are gone.

FIRST WORKER

Then we are free to go?

BRIGGS

Yes. It is so.

(BRIGGS escorts the workers out MARION
  remains behind. IAN speaks to her.)

IAN

For all I've failed,
I have made my confession,
Though I'll be jailed,
I'll honor my profession.
I'll march no more.
Within the mute procession,
My voice will roar
Against outside oppression.

MARION

Then I must share
A part of your contrition,

And I will dare
To fight this malnutrition.
My brother lives
As just an apparition,
One that forgives
My causing his condition.

IAN
It was I who hid atop a shelf.

MARION
That's not true.

IAN
It has been said,
His spirit can't be broken.

MARION
But if he's dead,
For words I should have spoken . . .
Then I'm the one
Whose spirit shall be broken,
For, what you've done
Is more than a kind token.

(The GENERAL begins to escort MARION away.)

IAN
Marion, I know your brother's fate.

MARION
Tell me so.

IAN

(Turning her away from the GENERAL so that they
can speak privately. GENERAL BRIGGS permits
them a moment alone.)

Yes, quickly, before it's too late.
Then you'll go.
You must see Brianna.
She's made a deal.

MARION

Then she will betray you
As she betrayed Neil.

So, you've struck a bargain
With the lady in red?
Was it consummated
When you went to her bed?

IAN

No, she is not my lover.
You'll find that she has changed.
We could free your brother
With what we've arranged.

MARION

Then he is still alive?

IAN

As far as I can tell.

MARION

Then you've traded places

And you will take his cell.
But what could be your reason?

IAN
I'm sorry, you must go.

MARION
But I must know your reason.

IAN
Because I love you so.
(They are spotlighted as he holds her hands
 and speaks.)

IAN
I'm a man who was lost in a barren mine
Where the pathway out was so labyrinthine.
And, were it not for you, I would still be there
Lost inside myself and afraid to care.

In your eyes was the only light to be seen,
And the face of hope was this sweet colleen.
And I wanted to tell you for such a long while,
But all I could do was return your smile.

Oh Marion, my dear Marion,
For so long I have watched you from afar.
Oh Marion, my dear Marion,
The night is gone, you're my morning star.

(they kiss)
It was easy to say it was my own choice,
But, when I tried to speak, I had no voice.

And so, they questioned my courage and my will,
They laughed at the hermit upon the hill.

Building bars in my mind, I lived in a cage,
Still, I made love to you on the written page.
And I'm sorry for all that I didn't do,
But regret not the road that led to you.

Oh Marion, my dear Marion,
For so long I have watched you from afar.
Oh Marion, my dear Marion,
The night is gone, you're my morning star.

(BRIGGS ENTERS and leads MARION off as
scene fades to black.)

(End of Scene 1.)

ACT II

Scene 2

SETTING: That night, MARION confronts BRIANNA at her cottage.

MARION
How many times
We've tangled in my head.
At last I meet
The lady in red.

How many times
In nightmares I've designed,
I've sought the truth,
To bring me peace of mind.

My brother's fate,
I want it on your lips!
I want your neck
Between my fingertips.

I've always been
A woman who loves peace,
But I am no more,
At least, 'til his release.

BRIANNA
For the deeds I have done
There can be no excuse.

I know I am the one
Who has caused this abuse.

But there's more to the tale
That goes beyond my acts.
Just open up your heart
And you will learn the facts.

General Briggs had threatened all my kin.
I played his game thinking that Neil would win.

MARION
You're beginning to sound
Like a Judas to me.

BRIANNA
Please, there isn't much time,
Or he'll never be free.

I hold the cash,
Ian's part of the deal.
It's all he has
To buy freedom for Neil.

MARION
And what becomes
Of Ian in that case?

BRIANNA
He takes Neil's cell
So, Briggs can save some face.

But once Neil's out,

Our flag will be unfurled,
And Ian's poems
Will finally tell the world.

(BRIANNA hands MARION a book.)

This is his book,
You must give it to Neil.
Ian in jail
Will give it more appeal.

MARION
Now the last romantic
Has his pen for a sword,
But his freedom's a price
That I cannot afford.

To feel such joy
And still to be so sad,
Ian for Neil;
I've given all I had.
And what shall Ian tell the world?

Fade to black.

(End Scene 2.)

ACT II

Scene 3

SETTING: IAN is now in the cell which was formerly occupied by NEIL. He speaks as if making a forceful political speech.

IAN
There are tables rich with bounty,
Within houses in the night,
Beneath the stars that bear witness
To what's in and out of sight.

They see children who are hungry
Down below them being fed,
Beneath rooftops that enclose them
In a warm and cozy bed.

They see cupboards that are empty,
And warehouses that are full,
Beneath those that broker power
With a simple latch to pull.

They see people who are dying
For the words we fear to say,
For to speak about this hunger
There's a bitter price to pay.

But, if we could just take the dare,
And risk our lives because we care,

We'd know a joy beyond compare.
It comes from giving,
And not from taking,
It's the joy of the bread we share.

(GENERAL BRIGGS ENTERS. He strikes
IAN in the back of the legs with a cudgel,
bringing him to his knees.)

BRIGGS
So, you have the gift of gab,
A way with words.
But once you sleep on a slab
Eat like the birds.

We'll see what you have inside
Left to protest.
We'll see who will be denied,
Who'll pass the test.

IAN
What I do, I do for love,
And love is its own glory.
Yet I pray to God above
The world will hear my story.

BRIGGS
We'll see how you like the rain,
Survive the cold,
We'll see if you go insane
Before you're old.

And how slowly years can pass,

How painfully,
And how much you'll miss the lass
You'll never see.

IAN
What I do, I do for love,
And love is its own glory.
Yet I pray to God above
The world will hear my story.

BRIGGS
There's the chance you might relapse
Before the end,
Take to drinking with, perhaps,
A little friend.

(As BRIGGS EXITS the cell, he rolls a whiskey
bottle across the floor to IAN, thinking that he's
tempting him to break his vow of sobriety. Timidly,
as if he were handling a snake, IAN picks up
the bottle and contemplates what to do.)

IAN
        (to himself.)
This is not my problem.

(ENTER DEVLIN)

DEVLIN
(Appearing suddenly, from under the bunk of
  the cell.)
There's the click
Of a key

Through the bars
You can see
Your old buddy.

IAN
(Referring to DEVLIN)
He is!

DEVLIN
Suddenly,
What was clear,
Will now seem
To appear
Rather muddy.

You won't eat,
You're on strike,
But I'm sure
You would like
To have freedom.

All you need
To be freed
Is to weed
Out the seed
Of your problem.

And everyone's got a potential pot of gold
A little trinket of a secret that they hold.
And just when you think you've found it,
Suddenly it's gone.
You never blame yourself,
You blame the leprechaun.

'tis the thing
That you crave
That can make
You behave
As I command.

DEVLIN
(continued)
I can smile,
I can wink,
I can watch
As you sink
Into quicksand.

You'll forget
What you fight,
And the poems
You could write
Won't see production.

You were cute
Little mute
In pursuit
Of the route
Of destruction.

But everyone's got a potential pot of gold.
A little trinket of a secret that they hold.
And just when you think you've found it,
Suddenly it's gone.
You never blame yourself,
You blame the leprechaun.

(DEVLIN attempts to run out of the cell but
  IAN takes his arm forcefully.)

IAN
There are reasons I made this exchange,
I can't forget them.
And there are things I cannot change,
I must accept them.
And those that I can rearrange,
I must perfect them.
And those that made me someone strange,
I must reject them.

In a time, not so long ago,
When I was so young,
There was a wee friend I used to know,
We spoke the same tongue.
He was a fantasy, I know,
A dream so far flung.
He helped my climb up, even so,
Up to the top rung.

IAN
(continued)
Did you know you were that friend
Until you became perverse?
Now we meet here at the end
Of what I can't reverse.

DEVLIN
But I've always been your friend.
What did you want of me?
I was your way to pretend.

I am your poetry.

(Fade to black.)

(End of Scene 3.)

ACT II

Scene 4

SETTING: In the yard outside the jail. NEIL and MARION are reunited, they embrace.)

NEIL
I'm here at last, in the place I've dreamed of.
I was sustained by my sister's sweet love.

MARION
You survived because of your own courage.
A love for man that no one could discourage.

NEIL
Perhaps that's why I still can't taste freedom,
For they still keep Ian in their prison.
I know I was captured by my failing,
For my lust led me to my own jailing.

(BRIANNA ENTERS)

BRIANNA
Not just your lust,
But, perhaps, your love.
(She attempts to touch NEIL. He recoils.)
Forgive me, before I meet God above.

MARION
Like you, I had the same reaction.

But I believe she regrets her action.

BRIANNA
Not just for us, but to end the famine,
There's a plan I want you to examine.
Not just for lust,
But, perhaps, for love,
Forgive me before I meet God above.

NEIL
For Ian, for the famine,
I'll listen to the plan.

BRIANNA
England knows little about the trade.
They think that an even swap was made.
The King never received Ian's wealth,
The general kept it for himself.

(MARION hands NEIL a letter)

MARION
This letter contains all of the facts.
For the general, it means the ax.
Take it tonight through the underground,
We have a place where it won't be found.

BRIANNA
I'll break the news to General Briggs,
He knows what makes kings flip their wigs.
Then I'll tell him; no one has to know,
So long as he will let Ian go.

NEIL
        (to BRIANNA)
You take the letter, I'll make the deal.

BRIANNA
There's still something for me you feel?
But I'm the one who's captured his trust . . .
Not just for love, not even for lust.

(BRIANNA attempts to take NEIL's hand as
BRIGGS and his SOLDIERS enter. BRIGGS
takes the letter from NEIL.)

BRIGGS
Isn't this all terribly quaint?
Enter a sinner, leave a saint.
Sorry, but I simply cannot
Allow you to play out this plot.

(BRIGGS dispatches his men to shackle
the three, then he speaks to NEIL.)
You will go back into your cell.
(to BRIANNA)
You'll be thrown down into a well.
(to MARION)
I will keep the last of the three,
I hope you'll enjoy slavery.

NEIL
Not so fast, my dear general.
You're just a common criminal.
I learned of all this yesterday,
Another letter left today.

It's time you set Ian free,
You can give his ransom to me.
Let us go back to our farm
(pointing to BRIANNA)
Take the shackles off of her arm.

BRIGGS
I am no more a general,
Now I am a common criminal.
I cannot let you just walk away,
One among you has to pay.

(BRIGGS has his men remove the shackles and
then motions for them to exit. When they do,
he turns to leave, but then spins and shoots
BRIANNA.)

BRIANNA
Not just for lust,
But also, for love,
Forgive me before I meet God above.

(BRIANNA dies in NEIL's arms.)

NEIL
I'd forgiven you
Long before you asked.

(Fade to black.)

(End of Scene 4.)

ACT II

Scene 5

SETTING: Later that day at the prison. MARION and NEIL free IAN from his cell unopposed. IAN stands with difficulty from his prison ordeal.

MARION
(To IAN)
Oh, lonesome man on a hermit's hill,
Speak ye now, or you never, ever, will.
Read a poem for the suffering souls,
It's for the likes of us that the church bell tolls.

(MARION and IAN embrace.)

IAN
Oh Marion, my dear Marion,
For so long I have watched you from afar.
Oh Marion, my dear Marion,
The night is gone, you're my morning star.

NEIL
        (embracing IAN.)
You're free to read your poetry,
Read it loud,
About hunger and poverty,
Before the crowd.

MARION
So not another family
Will have to choke.
We have our freedom finally,
In one bold stroke.

(IAN struggles to stand unaided. He finally
does so and moves down in 'one'.)

IAN
There are tables rich with bounty,
Within houses in the night,
Beneath the stars that bear witness
To what's in and out of sight.

They see children who are hungry,
Down below them being fed,
Beneath rooftops that enclose them
In a warm and cozy bed.

They see cupboards that are empty,
And warehouses that are full,
Beneath those that broker power,
With a simple latch to pull.

They see people who are dying
For the words we fear to say,
For to speak about this hunger,
There's a bitter price to pay.

(The full COMPANY enters as the lights
  come up. They stand arm-in-arm.)

But, if we would just take the dare
And risk our lives because we care,
We'd know a joy beyond compare.
It comes from giving
And not from taking,
It's the joy of the bread we share.

There are kingdoms green with envy
For the things they cannot buy,
Like an old man's wit and wisdom,
And the twinkle in his eye.

There's a kingdom green with beauty
That was painted by the hand,
That builds castles out of feelings
Inside every grain of sand.

They can't starve us of our courage,
Take iron from our soul,
'Though their sun may go on shining,
It is not theirs to control.

There are people who'll be living,
For the words we dare to say,
For to die to save the hungry,
We'll be born another day.

But, if we could just take the dare
And risk our lives because we care,
We'd know a joy beyond compare.
It comes from giving
And not from taking,
It's the joy of the bread we share.

MARION
There's a common dream
We share to be free,
For this magic place
To find unity.

NEIL
It's the force of God
No man can reverse,
Ireland has its place
In the universe.

ALL
Another chance,
And that is all we ask.
Another chance,
And we will meet the task.
Another chance,
And we will right the wrong.
Another chance
To raise one voice in song
For Ireland.

(End of Act II.)

(Curtain.)

About the Author

Edward Kenny recently published Bluebird Songs – Volume I., a book of lyrics and poems. *Lonesome Man on Hermit's Hill* is his first published verse play. Ed has written over a thousand song lyrics and eight musicals. He first entered the Broadway scene in 1982, when *Valhalla,* a musical he co-wrote with his longtime collaborator, composer/arranger Val Angrosini, received a first-class option. Material from the show was aired on television in conjunction with the *Hempkompst* expedition, a recreated Viking dragon ship which sailed from New York Harbor to Oslo, Norway. "*Valhalla*" was previewed by *Broadway Tomorrow Musical Theatre*, and was selected as a finalist in the New York drama league grants competition. The New York foundation for the arts awarded a grant to present *"Valhalla"* as a performance art work.

The World Goes On, a song from *Valhalla*, was aired on WGBB 1240, where Val and Ed were interviewed. At that time, two songs that they had written to commemorate the tragic events of September 11, 2001 were played, along with other original material.

Two additional musicals by this writing team, *Goodnight St. Petersburg* and *Straight to the Ace,* were also previewed by *Broadway Tomorrow*. Material from the shows was also aired on the New York City cable television talk/variety show *What's Going On,* where Val and Ed appeared as guests.

Straight to the Ace was nominated for the *Dramatists Guild* musical theatre program. It was also nominated by the *American Academy of Arts and Letters* for the *Harold Prince Musical Theatre* program. *Purple Cow Playhouse,*

Ltd. presented the show under a grant from the New York State Council on the Arts. *Ace* was also presented in *New York City* by Craig Slivka at the *Chelsea Playhouse, The Producer's Club, "The John Houseman Studio Theatre II, Theatre 22, The Home Theatre,* and the *Frederick Lowe Room of the Dramatists Guild.*

The Angrosini/Kenny collaboration began in 1979. The two have penned hundreds of songs which have been performed by Val's original bands at *The Right Track Inn, Paulson's, Catch a Rising Star, The Brokerage,* and other metropolitan area clubs, and recently, throughout central Florida. Their theme song for the group ***Amethyst*** was aired on television commercials.

Ed was a finalist in the Babylon citizens' council on the arts (BACCA) annual songwriting competition. His original songs have been aired on WUSB and WGBB radio, and on the television series *PM Magazine*. He studied poetry and lyric writing while attaining his Bachelor's Degree at Adelphi University.